TO THE RIVER
Odds and Probabilities in Texas Hold'em Poker

Sam Habash

iUniverse, Inc.
Bloomington

To the River
Odds and Probabilities in Texas Hold'em Poker

iUniverse books may be ordered through booksellers or by contacting:

iUniverse
1663 Liberty Drive
Bloomington, IN 47403
www.iuniverse.com
1-800-Authors (1-800-288-4677)

Because of the dynamic nature of the Internet, any Web addresses or links contained in this book may have changed since publication and may no longer be valid. The views expressed in this work are solely those of the author and do not necessarily reflect the views of the publisher, and the publisher hereby disclaims any responsibility for them.

Any people depicted in stock imagery provided by Thinkstock are models, and such images are being used for illustrative purposes only.

Certain stock imagery © Thinkstock.

ISBN: 978-1-4502-8435-6 (pbk)
ISBN: 978-1-4502-8437-0 (cloth)
ISBN: 978-1-4502-8436-3 (ebk)

Printed in the United States of America

iUniverse rev. date: 12/30/10

Contents

Introduction

This book is written for Texas Hold'em players, novice to expert, who would like to increase their knowledge of the game. This book is not intended to replace the basic poker skills, gut instincts, or typical luck of the draw required to win a poker tournament, but instead it provides the player with statistical probabilities on the possible outcome of the cards.

You have seen it on TV or played with a friend or in a casino: a player with an Ace/King hand usually raises the blinds or goes all in. But what is the probability of having an Ace or King show up in the hand? If you have a pair in your hand, what is the probability of getting a set, what is the probability of flopping two pair? Completing a straight or flush on the turn or river? This book will cover all of these questions and more.

The game of poker has been played for many years. Texas Hold'em, one of many variations of the game, has also been played for many years. But only recently has that variant achieved a huge following, with so many great, young players and worldwide tournaments. The inception of online play has also played a major role in the increase of the game's popularity. With so many websites now available, a novice fan can download one of any number of a pokers program and begin playing with either real or play money.

Yes, there are many excellent books already out there that cover the subject of poker. Most of them are written by professional poker players, and those books usually offer different strategies for winning. However, this book is slightly different, as it provides the reader with the mathematical probabilities of the possible outcomes for all scenarios of hands playing out, thus providing you with that additional tool and advantage. Over the last two to three years of playing the game, I began to calculate the probabilities of certain outcomes. I found this information very helpful in assisting me to place my bets or make folds or raises, or even when to go all in. I am certain that you will find this information helpful in making your decisions, as well.

This book also provides the reader with insight into the calculation of payback numbers—the ratio of pot size to the bet size compared to your odds of winning. Simply put, for example, if you are on a draw and your odds of winning are 25%, the pot size should be four times (or higher) than the bet size for it to be statistically sound to make the call.

To go deeper into an example of payback numbers, if you are on a flush draw after the flop, the probability of completing the flush on the turn or river is approximately 39%. The payback number will be (100 / 39), which is approximately two-and-one-half to one (or 2.5:1). So the pot size has to be two-and-one-half times the size of the bet to make it mathematically feasible for you to call. For you to call a $10 bet, the pot size should be at least $25.

As an additional feature, this book provides you with examples of most of the typical hands you will come across in a poker session. These examples are provided in a format with the hand shown after the flop and cover two very different, distinct scenarios:

- Examples of where you are playing high cards or pocket pairs and appear to be in the lead after the flop. These examples will provide you with the probabilities of someone having a better hand (a higher kicker, two pair, three of a kind, etc.).

- Examples of where you are basically on a draw and looking to improve your hand. These examples will provide you with the probabilities of completing your hand (straight, flush, full house, etc.).

I certainly hope you enjoy this book and that this probability information provides you with the slightest advantage in your next game or tournament. See you out there.

Chapter One

Getting Started

The game of Texas Hold'em poker is played in two major varieties, limit or no-limit. In limit poker, the casino or a house rule determines the bet limits (in terms of size) and number of allowed raises. No-limit poker is obviously very simple—there are no limits on any of the bets.

The game of Texas Hold'em is typically played with between six and ten players. Each player is dealt two down cards. To induce the betting, the two players to the left of the dealer are required to blind bet, and these are referred to as the small and big blinds. In addition to the two down cards (also called player cards), the dealer reveals five community cards, which are used by all players. These community cards will be opened at three different stages in order to induce betting.

Each player looks to make the best poker hand they can using any five of the seven total cards.

The Betting Process

There are four rounds of betting total:

First bet   **Made after the dealing of the player cards**

- The small and big blinds are bet automatically, before the dealing of the cards
- Betting here is induced by the blinds
- Players must match or raise the big blind

Second bet   **Made after revealing of the flop** (which consists of three community cards that are opened together)

- Bet sizes can vary depending on the game but can be from a minimum of the size of big blind to a maximum of the declared limit, or no limit

Third bet   **Made after revealing the turn card** (the fourth card of five community cards)

Fourth bet   **Made after revealing the river card** (the fifth card of the community cards)

Please note that any player can bet at any time, but betting is typically done in a sequential order starting to the left of the dealer.

Dependent Probabilities

In order to clarify some of the probability calculations in the book, I will briefly attempt to explain the theory of dependent probabilities and difference between those and non-dependent probabilities.

A player who is looking to flop a set (the common term for three of a kind) can do so if he has a pair in his hand that matches a card that comes on the flop. The probability of this is as follows:

Probability of being dealt a pocket pair 6%
Probability of matching a set on the flop 12.2% (2/50 × 3 = 12.2%)
 (2 out of 50 cards, and given three opportunities)

 Total of above probability 0.73% (less than one percent)

As you can see, the probability of starting with a pocket pair and the probability of matching the set on the flop had to be multiplied by each other to get the final probability. First you have to get a pair (probability 6/100) then match a card on the flop (12/100), with the overall probability being about .007 (seven hands out of one thousand). This is the concept of dependent probability. The first event has to happen in order for the second event to occur.

But since we all get to see our player cards, if you have already been lucky and have been dealt a pair in your hand, the probability of getting a set is on the flop will be **12.2%** because you've already got the pocket pair. Therefore, the probability of matching a set over the entire course of the hand is as follows:
 On the flop = 12.2%
 On the turn = 4.2%
 On the river = 4.3%
 Total 20.6%

So the probability of matching a pocket pair and getting a set is about 20%. But if you don't match it on the flop or the turn, the probability of matching it on the river is about 4%.

The probabilities are not dependent on each other since you got to see the card at each stage.

Payback Numbers

The payback number is the ratio of pot size to bet size. You will see this number throughout this book. The question the payback number helps you answer is, should you make that call on the turn or river card? The answer depends on the probability of your winning the hand.

Simply put, say you are on a draw and that your chances of winning the hand are 25%. In this case, the payback number is four to one, which is (100 / 25) and is also written as 4:1. Since your chances of winning are only 25%, you should be getting 4:1 odds in order to make your gamble mathematically worthwhile.

So just to clarify, if you are calling a $10 bet here and your chases of winning is 25%, the pot has to be at least 4 times the size of the bet.

As another example, if you believe that you have to match a set on the river (meaning you have a pocket pair in your hand) and you need to hit a set on the river to win.

The probability is   4.3%
so the payback number is   (100 / 4.3) = 23.2

so the pot-size-to-bet ratio has to be minimum of 23 to 1.

This means that if your competitor's bet was $10, the pot size has to be at least $230 to make this call mathematically feasible for you. So if the pot was much bigger than that, you should make the call, but if it was smaller than $230, then mathematically it is not wise.

Here is one more example: You are on a flush draw after the flop. The probability of completing the flush is 39%. Therefore, the payback number is approximately 2.5:1. So the pot size has to be two-and-one-half times the size of the bet to make calling mathematically feasible.

However, we all know that sometimes we are pot committed, depending on total stack situation and the size of the blinds. Remember, this book does not tell you what to do; it only provides you with the mathematical probabilities. The rest is up to you.

Chapter Two

Player Cards

I will not spend too much time on this subject, since most of the bidding in Texas Hold'em is done after the players review their cards. However, it is interesting to know certain probabilities, such as that of being dealt an Ace/King starting hand, or a pair.

Probability of having a pair	5.9%
Probability of having a combination of high cards (any combination of Aces and face cards)	7.2%
Total	13.1%

So as can be seen from above, the probability of getting a pair or any combination of high cards is around 13%. This means that if you are a player who plays only starting hands that consist of a combination of high cards or a pair, you will probably play around thirteen hands out of each one hundred dealt to you.

The probability of finding an Ace in the deck of cards is 1 in 52, or 7.7%, and that same probability applies to any specific card. So what is the probability of the following card combinations being dealt to you? Let's look at pairs, for example:

A. Pair of Aces   **0.45%**

For every two hundred hands played, you will get a pair of Aces once.

B. Any high pair   **1.8%**

(Aces, Kings, Queens, or Jacks)

C. Any pair higher than nines   **2.7%**

You will get a pair of Tens or higher in one out of every thirty-seven hands.

D. Any pair   **5.9%**

Now look at the probabilities of high card combinations:

A. Ace/King   **1.2%**

(also called "big slick")   As can be seen, getting Ace/King is about twice as likely as getting a pair of Aces.

B. Ace/any face card combination   **1.9%**

C. Any combination of high cards   **7.2%**

(Ace or face cards)   Slightly higher probability than getting any pair.

D. Combination of high cards suited   **1.1%**

(Ace and a face card suited)

Now we will look at the probability of opening with suited or connected cards:

A. Two suited cards   **23%**

B. Two suited and connected cards   **3.9%**

C. **Two high suited and connected cards**   1.2%
   (Jack and higher).

D. **Two high connected cards**   6.0%
   (cards higher than Ten)

Player Cards: Calculation Notes

Pairs:

A. Probability of a pair of Aces
    $(4 / 52) \times (3 / 51)$

    $= .077 \times .058$
    $= .0045$
    $= 0.45\%$

B. Any high pair
    (Aces, Kings, Queen, Jacks)

    $(16 / 52) \times (3 / 51)$

    $= .307 \times .059$
    $= .018$
    $= 1.8\%$

C. Any pair higher than nines

    $(24 / 52) \times (3 / 51)$

    $= .461 \times .059$
    $= .027$
    $= 2.7\%$

D. Any pair

    $1 \times (3 / 51)$

    $= .059$
    $= 5.9\%$

High card combinations:

A. Ace/King combination

    $(8 / 52) \times (4 / 51)$

    $= .153 \times .078$
    $= .012$
    $= 1.2\%$

B. Ace with any face card

    $(4 / 52) \times (12 / 51)$

    $= .076 \times .255$
    $= .019$
    $= 1.9\%$

C. Any combination of high cards
    (Ace or face cards)

    $(16 / 52) \times (12 / 51)$

    $= .307 \times .255$
    $= .072$
    $= 7.2\%$

D. Ace/face card combination suited

$(4 / 52) \times (3 / 51)$

$= .019 \times .059$
$= .0011$
$= 1.1\%$

Suited or Connected Cards
A. Two suited cards
$1 \times 12/51$
$= 23.5\%$

B. Two suited and connected cards
(Define connected as card next in sequence)
$1 \times 2/51$
$= 3.9\%$

C. Two high suited and connected cards
$16/52 \times 2/51$
$= 1.2\%$

CHAPTER THREE

One Pair

Now the player cards have been dealt, and you have a high-card combination, what is the probability of getting one pair or two pair? What is the probability of hitting a set, a straight draw, or a flush draw on the flop?

From this point forward, we will always be discussing probabilities after the players have reviewed their hands. We will also analyze the probabilities at three different stages:

1. Before the flop (three community cards)
2. Before the turn (fourth community card)
3. Before the river (fifth community card)

Since these stages are the betting points and the cards are revealed at each stage, we will also discuss the payback ratio (pot-size-to-final-bet-size) to determine the mathematical feasibility of calling on the river.

Probability of One Pair

With each player receiving two cards, the probability of one player getting one pair is as follows:

1. At the flop   36.7%
2. At the turn   12.7%
3. At the river   13.0%

Total probability of getting one pair: 62.3%

As can be seen from above, the probability of matching one pair is very high, so if you are a player that awaits high-card combination to play, your probability of making a high pair is six hands out of ten.

For example, if you are playing an Ace/Queen opening hand, the probability of getting an Ace or Queen is as follows:

On the flop
(6 outs / 50 cards) × 3 cards to be opened = 36.7%

On the turn
(6 outs / 47 cards) × 1 card to be opened = 12.7%

On the river
(6 outs / 46 cards) × 1 card to be opened = 13.0%

So the total probability of getting one pair is 36.7% + 12.7% + 13.0% = 62.3%.

Now you must note that the probability of matching one card only will be half of the above. So if you are playing a high card and a low card, such as Ace/Five or King/Four, the probability of matching the high card only is exactly half of the above.

Payback Information

Consider the scenario in which you are playing two high cards and you have not matched a pair through the turn, but you think you can win the hand with one pair (by matching on the river). The payback is as follows:

Playing an Ace/Queen hand, the probability of hitting an Ace or a Queen on the river is 13%.

Payback Ratio: (100 / 13) = **7.7:1**

So if the bet is $10.00, the pot size should be a minimum of $77.00 to make calling mathematically feasible.

Summary

The probability getting one pair on the flop is 36.6%. If you have high cards in your hand and you did not match a pair on the flop, the probability now of getting one pair on the turn or river is around 25%.

Remember, the total probability of getting one pair is 62.3%, meaning that just over six times out of ten, your opponent will also make a pair.

If there are a total of five players in a hand (you plus four opponents), and assuming that there are eight different cards dealt, the probability of someone having a pair is 8 out of 13. So with five players, (8 / 13) = 61.5% that one of your opponents has made a pair.

Your probability of catching a pair on the river is 13%, and the payback is approximately 7.7:1. This means that the pot has to be more than eight times the size of the bet to make calling feasible.

One Pair: Calculation Notes

Probability of one pair on the flop: three opportunities, six outs for each opportunity:

$(6 / 50) + (6 / 49) + (6 / 48)$

$= .120 + .122 + .125$
$= .367$
$= 36.7\%$

On the turn, one opportunity:

$6 / 47$

$= .127$
$= 12.7\%$

On the river, one opportunity:

$6 / 46$

$= .130$
$= 13.0\%$

CHAPTER FOUR

Two Pair

There are many ways of getting two pair.

A. **On the flop**

The probability of matching two pair right at the flop is **2.23%**.

If you are playing a hand of Ace/Queen, just for example, the probability of matching two pair at flop is as follows:

You can match the first pair (either Ace or Queen, six outs) on the first card, then you have three outs, but two opportunities to match the second pair.

$$(6 / 50) \times ((3 / 49) + (3 / 48)) = \mathbf{1.47\%}$$

If you did not match either card on the first card, then you have to match the first pair on the second card and second pair on the third card. You have three outs to be matched on the second card and then also three outs on the third card.

$$1 \times (3 / 49) \times (3 / 48) = \mathbf{0.75\%}$$

Add those together. **Total probability = 2.23%**

B. One pair on the flop, the second on the turn or river

The probability of matching one pair at the flop, as discussed in Chapter Three, is 36.7%.

Second pair on the turn   = 6.4%
Second pair on the river   = 6.5%

So if you had one pair on the flop, the total probability of getting a second pair is at **12.9%**. Your **payback number** will be **7.5:1**.

C. No pair after the flop

Probability of getting first pair on the turn   = **12.5%**
Probability of getting second pair on the river   = **6.5%**

Total probability of getting two pair after flop   = **0.8%**

D. The board pairing up on the flop

In this scenario, the first card could be any card, and there are two opportunities to match it. If the second card does not match the first card, there is still one opportunity to match on the third card. The calculations are as follows:

$1 \times ((3 / 49) + (3 / 48))$ = **12.3%**

$1 \times 1 \times (3 / 48)$ = **6.25%**

Total probability   = **18.5%**

So the probability of any pair showing up on the flop is **18.5%**.

E. The board pairing up on the turn or the river

What is the probability of the board pairing up on the turn or river? Sometimes this is very important, such as if you are holding a set and need the board to pair up to make a full house.

Any three cards come on the flop. The probability of matching a pair:

On the turn, you have nine outs to match any of the three cards on the flop.

9 / 47 = 19.1%

On the river, now there are twelve outs to match any card on the board.

12 / 46 = 26.0%

Total probability   = **45.1%**

So just remember, there is a 45% chance that the board will pair up after the flop.

Probability of Two Pair

A. The probability of getting two pair right on the flop is very low, **2.25%**. However, there is a high probability that this hand will improve dramatically (see the chapter on full houses).

B. The probability of getting one pair on the flop is **36.5%**. (If you are lucky and have indeed flopped a pair). The probability of getting a second pair on the turn or river is at 12.5%.

C. If you have a high pair in your hand, the probability of a pair showing up on the flop is **18.5%**.

Above all else, remember that the probability of the board pairing up after the flop is very high, about 45% of the time.

Two Pair: Calculation Notes

A. Two pair on the flop

You match either one of your player cards on the first card, then you have two opportunities to match the second card.

$$(6 / 50) \times ((3 / 49) + (3 / 48)) = 1.47\%$$

If you miss the first card on the flop, then you must match the first pair on the second card and second pair on the third card.

$$1 \times (6 / 49) \times (3 / 48) = 0.076\%$$

Total probability   = 2.23%

B. One pair on the flop, second pair on the turn or river

If you have one pair on the flop, the probability of a second pair comes with two chances.

Second pair on the turn:
3 outs / 47 cards = 6.4%

Second pair on the river:
3 outs / 46 cards = 6.5%

CHAPTER FIVE

Three of a Kind

There are two ways to get three of a kind, also called a set:

A. **Getting a set starting with a pair in your opening hand**

On the flop = **12.2%**
On the turn = **4.2%**
On the river = **4.3%**

The total probability is **20.7%**

In summary, just remember that if you start with a pair in your hand, the probability of hitting a set on the flop is 12.2%, and the probability of hitting a set overall is 20.7%.

In reality, in most situations if you're holding a low pair in your hand, it is hard to call on the turn or river because the payback number is so high.

The probability of making a set on the turn is 8.5% because you have the chance from the turn card and another chance from the river card.

Because the probability of hitting three of a kind on the river is at **4.3%**, the payback number is 23:1. So if you think you need to hit three of a kind on the river to win the pot, the pot has to be at minimum twenty-three times size of a bet that you're up against to make it mathematically worthwhile.

B. **Getting a set without a pair in your opening hand**

For any two cards you are playing, the probability of getting a set on the flop is lower than getting a set when you start with a pair. Assume you are starting with a hand of Eight/Nine. What is the probability of having either two Eights or two Nines show up on the flop?

First card (either an Eight or a Nine): 6 outs / 50 cards
Second card (must match first card): 2 outs / 49 cards

$(6 / 50) \times (2 / 49) = .0049$, or **0.49%**

You have two chances, the second and third card, so the total probability of getting a set on the flop starting with any two cards is a total of **almost 1%**.

Now if you matched a pair on the flop, the probability of completing a set on the turn or river is as follows:

On the turn= 4.2% (2 outs / 47 cards)
On the river= 4.3% (2 outs / 46 cards)

Summary

A. You obviously have an advantage if you start with a pair in your hand. This makes your total probability of getting a set **21%**.

But if you have not matched a set after the turn, whether to call any bet becomes a good question—it might depend on how high your pair is. The probability of hitting a set on the river is only **4.3%**. That is a payback of 23:1.

B. The probability of getting a set on the flop with any two cards is at a total of **1%.**

The probability of getting a set on the turn or river after you have a pair on the flop is a total of **8.5%**, because the chance of making three of a kind at the turn is **4.2%**, and the chance on the river is **4.3%**.

Three of a Kind: Calculation Notes

A.   Starting with a pair in your hand (any of the cards on the flop match your pair):

The first card is two outs out of fifty cards, the second card is two outs out of forty-nine, and the third card gives you two outs out of forty seven cards:

$(2 / 50) + (2 / 49) + (2 / 48)$
$=$ $.04 + .041 + .041$
$=$ **12.2%**

B. Starting with any two cards in your hand:

If the first card matches any of the two cards in your hand, there are six outs in the deck.
       $= 6 / 50$

The second card **has** to match the first card, leaving only two outs.
       $= 2 / 50$

You have two chances to match the first card—either on the second or third card of the flop. This means the calculations are as follows:

$(6 / 50) \times (2 / 49) \times 1 = .049$
$(6 / 50) \times 1 \times (2 / 49) = .049$
Total $= .098$, or **almost 1%**

CHAPTER SIX

Straights

There are two distinct ways to make a straight in Texas Hold'em poker:

A. Using both cards from your starting hand

B. Using only one card from your starting hand

However, there are many different combinations to making the straight.

A. Using both cards from your starting hand

If you are starting out with two connected cards, such as Seven/Eight or Nine/Ten, there are four different combinations that can make you a straight on the flop. Let's consider an opening hand of Seven/Eight. For this you need one of the following flops:

6-9-10
5- 6- 9
4-5-6
9-10-J

The probability of flopping any of these combinations is .0031, or **0.31%**.

Here is the calculation. You require three specific cards, such as the 6-9-10 combination.

First card: any of the above cards   (12 / 50) = 24%
(There are four of each in the deck, thus there are twelve outs.)

Second card: any one of the other two cards in the straight (8 / 49) = 16%
(There are eight outs, four each of the two cards.)

Third card: must be the last of the three above   (4 / 48) = 8%
(There are four outs, four copies of the last card you need.)

So the total probability is $.24 \times .16 \times .08 = .0031$

However, since there are four combinations of three cards that will each work, the grand total probability is $.0031 \times 4 = \mathbf{1.2\%}$

So when you are starting with two connected cards, the probability of completing the straight on the flop is at 1.2%.

Please note that if you start with high-end connected cards (Ace/King or Ace/Two), your chances of making a straight are lower, since there is only one combination.

If you are starting with partially connected cards, such as Seven/Nine, Nine/Jack, or Eight/Ten, there are only three combinations of three cards that will make a straight. Thus the overall probability is **0.9%**

As can be seen, the probability of getting a straight on the flop is very low, less than 1%. Most straights are typically finished on the turn or river. There are two possibilities for this:

Open-ended straight on the flop

If you are playing, for example, a Nine/Ten hand and the flop is J-Q-4, the probability of completing a straight is **34.4%**.

You have two draws to finish it, the turn and river.

On the turn   = 17.0%
8 outs / 47 cards

On the river   = 17.4%
8 outs / 46 cards

The payback number on the river is 5.7:1, so for a $10 bet, the pot has to be a minimum of $57 dollars to make a call worthwhile.

Inside straight draw

If you have an inside straight draw after the flop, the probability of completing the straight is half the above because you only have half as many outs.

On the turn   = 8.5%
4 outs / 47 cards

On the river   = 8.7%
4 outs / 46 cards

Total   = 17.2%

The payback number on the river is 11.5:1, meaning for a $10 bet, the pot has to be a minimum of $115 dollars for you to be wise to call.

B. **Using only one card from your starting hand**

You cannot flop a straight using only one card from your hand. You might flop an open-ended or an inside straight draw, however, which you can then complete on the turn or the river.

For example, if you are playing a Ten/Four hand and the flop is 8-9-J, you have flopped an opened-ended straight.

The probability of such a flop is $(4 / 50) \times (4 / 49) \times (4 / 48)$

$$= .08 \times .081 \times .083$$
$$= 0.0005 \,\%$$

Very low odds.

The probability of completing the straight is the same as described in the section above.

CHAPTER SEVEN

Flushes

The flush is one of the most intriguing hands in poker, especially in limit games. Why? Because many players will chase a flush draw right to the river; typically, a flush will represent the winning hand.

A flush will usually be the best hand if the board does not pair up (though watch out for a possible straight flush hand). Typically, an Ace-high flush is the nuts—the best hand possible—when the board does not pair up.

A flush can be obtained in two ways:

A. Using two suited cards from your opening hand

B. Using one card from your opening hand and four suited cards on the board

We will examine scenario A first, as you have to be very lucky to hit a flush in scenario B—though it does happen frequently enough for us to provide you with the probability.

A. **Using two suited cards from your opening hand**

Earlier we have examined the probability of getting two suited cards in your opening hand (23%), but once you have two suited cards, here is the probability of completing the flush:

To get the flush on the flop, all three suited cards on the flop must match your suit.

The probability is $(11 / 50) \times (10 / 49) \times (9 / 48) = .0084$, or **just under 1%**

It is more likely you'll have a four-card flush on the flop and then hit the flush on the turn or river.

The probability of completing the flush on the turn of the river is **38.6%**.

Here is the calculation:

> On the turn
> 9 outs / 47 cards = 19.1%
>
> On the river
> 9 outs / 46 cards = 19.5%

Sum to get the total = 38.6%

Of note, this means that the probability of hitting this flush draw is slightly higher than the probability of completing an open-ended straight.

So in summary, if you have two suited cards, the probability of hitting the flush directly on the flop is just less than 1%.

But if you get to four cards to a flush, the probability of hitting the flush goes up considerably. Once you have a four-card flush draw after the flop, you will make the flush 38.6% of the time. Very good odds. That is why many players will raise when they hit a four-card flush on the flop.

Note that if you miss your flush card on the turn, the probability of hitting it on river will be a bit more than half what it was before, 19.5%.

If you have a four-card flush before the river, the payback number is (100 / 19.5) = 5.1:1.

That means that the pot has to be a minimum of five times the size of the last bet to make calling feasible. For a $10 bet, the pot size should be greater than $50 dollars.

B. Using one card from your opening hand

The probability that the board will have four cards of the same suit is described here. We will use an example starting hand of Ace of hearts and any non-heart card.

The probability of getting a three-heart at flop is:

(12 outs / 50 cards) × (11 / 49) × (10 / 48)
     24%   × 22.4%   × 20.8%   = **1.1%**

Those are low odds, but if you are lucky and you flopped three hearts, the probability of completing the flush is the same as for finishing a flush where you began with two suited cards, or 38.6%.

Flush with an open-ended straight draw

Consider if you have a hand like Jack/Ten, suited in clubs. If the flop is King of clubs-Queen of hearts-Four of clubs, the probability of getting a straight or a flush will be very high. You have 17 outs (nine cards to make the flush plus eight cards to make the straight):

On the turn   = 36.1%
17 outs / 47 cards

On the river   = 36.9%
17 outs / 46 cards

Added together = **73%**

So you can see that you have a 73% chance of completing either the flush or the straight. Very good odds.

The payback number going into the river is 2.7:1. For a $10 bet, the pot has to be greater than $27 dollars to make the call worthwhile.

Chapter Eight

Full House

There are three main different possibilities for getting a full house:

A. On the flop

B. Two pair on the flop, then full house on turn or river

C. Three of a kind on the flop, then full house on the turn or river

A. Full house on the flop

As you can imagine, the probability of getting a full house on the flop is very low. Starting with any two cards in your hand, the probability is **0.1%**.

Let's say your hand is Jack/Ten. You will need either J-J-10 or 10-10-J. The probability is as follows:

$(6 / 50) \times (5 / 49) \times (4 / 48)$
   $= .12 \times .012 \times .083$
   $= .001$, or one hand out of one thousand

Starting with a pair in your hand, the probability is **1%**.

For example, if you start with a pair of Jacks, you will need the flop to be a Jack and any pair combination. The probability is as follows:

$$1 \times (5 / 49) \times (5 / 48)$$
$$= .102 \times .104$$
$$= .01, \text{ or one hand out of one hundred}$$

B. Full house through two pair on the flop

The probability of getting two pair on the flop, as calculated earlier in the book, is around **2.25%**.

Remember the principle of dependent probabilities. Once you have two pair on the flop, you have already beaten the long odds. The probability of completing the full house is **17.2%**.

For example, again playing Jack/Ten, if the flop is J-10-A, you will need a Jack or Ten on the turn or river:

4 outs on the turn	4 / 47 = 8.5%
4 outs on the river	4 / 46 = 8.6%
	Total 17.2%

C. Full house through three of a kind on the flop

The probability of having three of a kind on the flop.
Pocket pair in your hand.
Probability of flopping a set =12.2%

But again, if you are lucky and flopped set or matched two of your player cards, the probability of completing the full house is at **25.7%**.

Here are two examples:

You are playing a Jack/Jack hand	or	You are playing an Eight/ Nine hand
The flop is J-8-6		The flop is 9-9-6

In both cases, you need to match either Eight or the Six (same odds both hands).

Turn	6 outs / 47 cards =	**12.7%**
River	6 outs / 46 cards =	**13.0%**
	Total =	**25.7%**

So if you flop three of a kind, the probability of completing a full house is 25.7%. This puts the payback number at 3.9:1

But remember, you already have a three of a kind! You probably should not fold unless you think you are losing to a straight or a flush.

Summary

A full house in Texas Hold'em poker is a very strong hand, considering you are playing with a total of seven cards only.

To recap, to flop a full house:
> Starting with a pair in your hand, the probability is **1%**.
> Starting with any two cards in your hand, the odds are **0.1%**.

If you hit two pair on the flop:
> The odds of completing a full house are **17.1%**; at the turn **8.5%** and at the river **8.6%**.

If you hit three of a kind on the flop:
> The odds of completing a full house are **25.7%**; at the turn **12.7%** and at the river **13.0%**.

CHAPTER NINE

Four of a Kind

The probability of getting four of a kind in Texas Hold'em is very low.
A. Starting with any two cards in your hand
Using the example of an Ace/Jack starting hand, you need to match either three Jacks or three Aces. The probability is as follows:

$(3 / 50) \times (2 / 49) \times (1 / 48)$ (three chances including the turn and river)
$= .06 \times .041 \times .062$
$= .00015\%$

But we have two cards either an Ace or Jack
Thus total probability of $.00015 \times 2 = .00030\%$.
That is thirty hands out of every one hundred thousand hands dealt, or one in nearly thirty three hundred hands.

B. Starting with a pair in your hand, the odds are a little higher.
For instance, if you start with a pair of Tens, you need to hit both remaining Tens in the deck. The probability is as follows:

$(2 / 50) \times (1 / 49)$ (but you have four chances)
$.04 \times (.02 \times 4)$

= .0032%

That is three hands out of one thousand.

When you have three of a kind on the flop, the probability of completing four of a kind is still low, at only **4.2%**.

Consider if you have Jack/Ten and the flop is J-J-2. The probability of the fourth Jack coming is:

On the turn   1 / 47 = **2.1%**
On the river   1 / 46 = **2.1%**
    Total   **4.2%**

CHAPTER TEN

Straight Flush

The probability of getting a straight flush in poker is extremely low, comparable to the odds of getting four of a kind.

You can make a straight flush. If you are playing two suited cards, for instance Jack/Nine of clubs, here is the probability of getting a straight flush, you will need the following:

First card: Ten of clubs

Second card: Any of the following, King, Queen, Seven, or eight of clubs.

Third/forth, Fifth card: You will need to complete the straight flush so if you hit the seven on the forth card, you'll need the eight of club, and if you hit the King you will need the Queen of clubs, thus one out only.

These are very specific cards corresponding to the following odds:

$(1 / 50) \times (4 / 49) \times 1/48 \times 3$ (three chances including the turn and river)

$.02 \times .081 \times (.02 \times 3)$

$= 0.000010\%$

That corresponds to about one out of every one hundred thousand hands played.

However, most times when players get a straight flush, they do so when they flop an open-ended straight flush draw. In this case the odds are **8.7%**.

Let's look at the calculation, assuming one is playing Jack/Ten of clubs. If the flop was K-Q of- clubs, the probability of completing a straight flush:

On the turn   (2 / 47) = .042 need either Ace or Nine of clubs
On the river   (2 / 46) = .043 need either Ace or Nine of clubs
    Total   = 0.087

So a total of 8 .7% chance of completing the straight flush

Finally, if you have an inside draw for a straight flush on the flop, the probability of completing it is **4.5%** half the chance of open ended draw.

CHAPTER ELEVEN

Examples

In this section of the book we will look at twenty of the most typical
hands played. But please note that the first ten examples have different
parameters from the second ten.

First Set of Examples (1–10)

These are examples of where you are playing high cards or pocket pairs
and appear to be in the lead after the flop. In these scenarios, you are
given the probability of someone having a better hand, such as three of
a kind, two pair, a higher kicker, and so on.

The probability provided to you in these examples is also based on the
number of players in the hand. For instance, if the flop is A-7-7 and
you have Ace/King, what is the mathematical probability of someone
having a Seven?

Second Set of Examples (11–20)

These are examples detailing situations when you are basically on a draw and looking to improve your hand, such as when you have top pair or a flush or straight draw. You are likely behind, and you need your hand to improve. Here we provide the probability of your hand improving in these different scenarios.

Altogether, these examples represent the majority of the situations you encounter while playing Texas Hold'em poker.

Summary of Examples 1–10

Your hand	Against
1. Top pair on the flop (There is a pair on the flop)	Possible set
2. High pocket pair (Kings)	One higher card on the flop (Ace on the flop)
3. Medium pocket pair (Tens)	Two higher cards on the flop
4. Top pair, low kicker	Higher kicker
5. Top pair, Seven kicker	Higher kicker
6. Top pair, Ten kicker	Higher kicker
7. Top pair, top kicker (Ace/King)	Two pair (Ace/low)
8. Top pair	Two pair
9. Low-end straight	High-end straight
10. Ten-high flush	Higher flush

These examples provide the probabilities of someone having you beat even when you have a good hand, which you think is the best hand. The examples calculate the mathematical probability based on the numbers of players still involved in the hand.

Example 1
Top pair against a possible set

Your hand
      ACE   KING
      DIAMONDS CLUBS

The flop
      ACE   SEVEN   SEVEN
      HEARTS   CLUBS   DIAMONDS

What is the probability of someone having a Seven in their hand?

Total of four players (including you), so three opponents: **25.5%**

    The probability of having a Seven is (2 / 47) = 4.2%
    There are six cards, three players times two cards each.
    6 × 4.2% = 25.5%

Total of three players (two opponents): **16.8%**

Total of two players (one opponent): **8.4%**

So you must note that with a total of three opponents there is a **25%** chance that someone has a Seven in their hand.

Example 2
High pocket pair against one higher card on the flop

Your hand
       KING   KING
       CLUBS   SPADES

The flop
      ACE   JACK   EIGHT
      HEARTS   SPADES   CLUBS

What is the probability of someone having an Ace in their hand?

Total of four players (including you), so three opponents: **38.4%**

    The probability of having an Ace is (3 / 47) = 6.4%
    There are six cards, three players times two cards each.
    6 × 6.4% = 38.4%

Total of three players (two opponents):   **25.6%**

Total of two players (one opponent):   **12.8%**

So you must note that with a total of three opponents there is about a 40% chance that someone will have an Ace in their hand.

Example 3
Medium pocket pair against two higher cards on the flop

Your hand
>TEN   TEN
>SPADES   DIAMONDS

The flop
>KING   JACK   SEVEN
>HEARTS   CLUBS   SPADES

What is the probability of someone having either a King or a Jack in their hand?

Total of four players (including you), so three opponents: **76.2%**

>The probability of having a King or Jack is (6 / 47) = 12.7%
>There are six cards, three players times two cards each.
>6 × 12.7% = 76.2%

Total of three players (two opponents):   **50.8%**

Total of two players (one opponent):   **25.4%**

So you must note that with a total of three opponents there is a 76.2% chance that someone will have either a King or a Jack in their hand.

Example 4
Top pair, low kicker

Your hand
ACE	TWO
HEARTS	CLUBS

The flop
ACE	JACK	EIGHT
CLUBS	DIAMONDS	SPADES

What is the probability of someone having an Ace in their hand with higher kicker than your Two?

The probability of hitting an Ace is (2 / 47) = 4.2%

In this scenario, your opponent has to have an Ace with a kicker higher than two.

Probability of first card being an Ace	4.2%
Probability of second card being any card higher than Two	(11 / 12) = .92

So the total probability would be 4.2% × .92 = 3.8%

This gives you the following probabilities:

Total of four players (three opponents): 3 × 3.8% = 11.4%	**11.4%**
Total of three players (two opponents):	**7.6%**
Total of two players (one opponent):	**3.8%**

So you must note that with a total of three opponents there is an 11.4% chance that someone will have an Ace with higher kicker than your Two.

Example 5
Top pair, Seven kicker

Your hand
      ACE   SEVEN
      HEARTS   CLUBS

The flop

      ACE   JACK   EIGHT
      CLUBS   DIAMONDS SPADES

What is the probability of someone having an Ace in their hand with higher kicker than your Seven?

Your opponent has to have an Ace with a kicker higher than Seven.
The probability of the first card being an Ace   4.2%
The probability of the second card being any card
higher than Seven   (6 / 12) = .50

    So the total probability would be 4.2% × .50 = 2.1%

This gives you the following probabilities:

Total of four players (three opponents):   **6.3%**
3 × 2.1% = 6.3%

Total of three players (two opponents):   **4.2%**

Total of two players (one opponent):   **2.1%**

So you must note that with a total of three opponents there is a 6.3% chance that someone will have an Ace with a higher kicker than your Seven.

Example 6
Top pair, Ten kicker

Your hand
        ACE   TEN
        HEARTS   CLUBS

The flop
        ACE   JACK   EIGHT
        CLUBS   DIAMONDS SPADE

What is the probability of someone having an Ace in their hand with higher kicker than your Ten?

Your opponent has to have an Ace with a kicker higher than Ten.

Probability of the first card being an Ace	4.2%
Probability of the second card being any card higher than Ten	(3 / 12) = .25

So the total probability would be 4.2% × .25 = 1.0%

This gives you the following probabilities:

Total of four players (three opponents):   **3.0%**
3 × 1.0% = 3.0%

Total of three players (two opponents):   **2.0%**

Total of two players (one opponent):   **1.0%**

So you must note that with a total of three opponents there is a 3.0% chance that someone will have an Ace with a higher kicker than your Ten.

Example 7
Top pair, top kicker against two pair

Your hand
>   ACE   KING
>   SPADES   HEARTS

The flop
>   ACE   SIX   TWO
>   CLUBS   DIAMONDS   SPADES

What is the probability of someone having two pair in their hand (Ace/ Two or Ace/Six)?

Your opponent has to have an Ace with a Six or Two.
Probability of the first card being an Ace   4.2%
Probability of the second card being a Six or Two $(6 / 47) = .13$

So the total probability would be $4.2\% \times .13 = 0.56\%$

This gives you the following probabilities:

Total of four players (three opponents):   **1.68%**
$3 \times 0.56\% = 1.68\%$

Total of three players (two opponents):   **1.12%**

Total of two players (one opponent):   **0.56%**

So you must note that with a total of three opponents there is a 1.68% chance that someone will have two pair (Aces with Sixes or Twos).

Example 8
Top pair against two pair

Your hand
     QUEEN   NINE
     SPADES   HEARTS

The flop
     QUEEN   EIGHT   SEVEN
     CLUBS   HEARTS   DIAMONDS

What is the probability of someone having two pair in their hand?

Your opponents could have any of these possible combinations: Queen/Eight; Queen/Seven; Eight/Seven

There are two outs to draw a Queen, three outs to draw an Eight, and three outs to draw a Seven:

8 outs × 6 outs
$(8 / 47) \times (6 / 46) = 2.2\%$

Total of four players (three opponents):   **6.6%**
$3 \times 2.2\% = 6.6\%$

Total of three players (two opponents):   **4.2%**

Total of two players (one opponent):   **2.2%**

So you must note that with a total of three opponents there is a 6.6% chance that someone will have two pair in their hand.

Example 9
Low-end straight against high-end straight

Let's look at this example after the turn:

Your hand
    EIGHT   SIX
    SPADES   HEARTS

The flop and turn
    NINE   TEN   JACK   QUEEN
    SPADES   CLUBS   HEARTS DIAMONDS

What is the probability of someone having a King in their hand?

Total of four players (including you), so three opponents: **51.0%**

    The probability of having a King is (4 / 47) = 8.5%
    There are six cards, three players times two cards each.
    6 × 8.5% = 51.0%

Total of three players (two opponents):   34.0%

Total of two players (one opponent):   17.0%

So with an open-ended straight there is 51% chance that against three players, someone will have the high-end straight.

Example 10
Ten-high flush against higher flush

Let's look at this example after the turn:

Your hand
TEN	NINE
CLUBS	HEARTS

The flop and turn
ACE	NINE	SIX	FOUR
CLUBS	CLUBS	CLUBS	CLUBS

What is the probability of someone having a higher club than your Ten in their hand?

There are three higher clubs remaining: King, Queen, and Jack.

Total of four players (including you), so three opponents: **38.4%**

The probability of having a higher club is (3 / 47) = 6.4%
There are six cards, three players times two cards each.
6 × 6.4% = 38.4%

Total of three players (two opponents):   **25.6%**

Total of two players (one opponent):   **12.8%**

So there is very good chance (almost 40%) that someone will have the higher flush. Note with only two higher cards than yours (and still against three players), the probability drops to 25%.

Summary of Examples 11–20

Your hand	Probability of completion (%)	Payback
11. High cards, looking for top pair on the turn or river	25.8	3.9:1
12. One pair, looking for second pair or set	21.4	4.7:1
13. Low pair in your hand, looking for set	8.5	11.8:1
14. Inside straight draw	17.1	5.8:1
15. Inside straight draw plus a pair	38.6	2.6:1
16. Open-ended straight draw	34.2	2.9:1
17. Flush draw	38.7	2.6:1
18. Flush draw plus a pair	60.1	1.6:1
19. Open-ended straight draw plus flush draw	73.0	1.4:1

20. Full house draw
   a) Two pair on the flop   23.7   4.2:1
   b) Set on the flop   32.3   3.1:1

This set of example hands is based on the draws you have after the flop. The probabilities provided are about completing your hand on the turn or river.

Please note that if you miss on the turn, the probability of completing on the river is about half the probability shown, and the payback numbers are doubled.

Example 11
High cards, looking for a pair on turn or river

Your hand
        ACE   KING
        DIAMONDS   CLUBS

The flop
        QUEEN   EIGHT   TWO
        DIAMONDS   HEARTS   SPADES

You missed the flop. You are assuming the best hand is a pair of Queens.

What is the probability of an Ace or King showing up on the turn or river?

You have six outs:

On the turn   (6 / 47) = 12.8%
On the river   (6 / 46) = 13.0%
    Total   = **25.8%**

So the total probability of your catching an Ace or King is 25.8%. Approximately 26% of the time you will get the top pair on the turn or river, so the Payback is 3.9:1
Payback calculations (100 / 25.8 = 3.9)

Example 12
One pair on the flop, looking for a second pair or set

Your hand
      NINE   SEVEN
      DIAMONDS   CLUBS

The flop
      QUEEN   JACK   NINE
      DIAMONDS   HEARTS   SPADES

You have one pair on the flop. What is probability of getting a second pair or set?

What is the probability of a Seven or Nine showing up?

You have five outs:

On the turn   (5 / 47) = 10.6%
On the river   (5 / 46) = 10.8%
   Total   = **21.4%**

So the total probability of your catching a Seven or Nine is 21.4%. The payback number is 4.7:1.

Example 13
Low pair in your hand, looking for a set

Your hand
      SIX   SIX
      DIAMONDS   CLUBS

The flop
      QUEEN   EIGHT   TWO
      DIAMONDS HEARTS   SPADES

You missed the flop. You are assuming the best hand is a pair of Queens.

What is the probability of a Six showing up?

You have two outs:

On the turn $(2 / 47) = 4.2\%$
On the river $(2 / 46) = 4.3\%$
    Total $= \textbf{8.5\%}$

So the total probability of your catching a Six and making your set is 8.5% (very low odds). The payback number, as expected, will be very high at 11.8:1. For a $10 bet, the pot has to be greater than $118 dollars to make calling a good decision.

Example 14
Inside straight draw

Your hand
QUEEN	TEN
DIAMONDS	CLUBS

The flop
JACK	EIGHT	SEVEN
DIAMONDS	HEARTS	SPADES

You have an inside straight draw, which you need a Ten to complete.

What is the probability of a Ten showing up?

You have four outs:

On the turn	(4 / 47) = 8.5%
On the river	(4 / 46) = 8.6%
Total	= **17.1%**

So the total probability of your catching a Ten on the turn or river is 17.1%. The payback number is 5.8:1.

Example 15
Inside straight draw plus a pair

Your hand
      TEN   SEVEN
      DIAMONDS   CLUBS

The flop
      JACK   EIGHT   SEVEN
      DIAMONDS   HEARTS   SPADES

You have an inside straight draw plus a low pair.

What is the probability of completing the straight, getting a second pair, or getting a set?

You have a total of nine outs:

Complete the straight Four outs (one of the Nines)
Complete the set Two outs (the remaining Sevens)
Second pair Three outs (the remaining Tens)

On the turn   (9 / 47) = 19.1%
On the river   (9 / 46) = 19.5%
   Total   = **38.6%**

So when you have an inside straight draw with a pair, the probability of improving your hand is much higher than having a straight draw alone, at a total of 38.6%. But you must note that if you match your second pair, that will open a four-card straight draw.

Payback number is at 2.6:1 (100 / 38.6 = 2.6)

Example 16
Open-ended straight draw

Your hand
>   QUEEN   TEN
>   DIAMONDS   CLUBS

The flop
>   KING   JACK   SIX
>   DIAMONDS   HEARTS   SPADES

You have an open-ended straight draw. You need either an Ace or Nine to complete it, so you have a total of eight outs:

On the turn   (8 / 47) = 17.0%
On the river   (8 / 46) = 17.2%
>   Total   = **34.2%**

So the total probability of your catching the straight is 34.2% (very good odds). The payback number is 2.9:1.

Example 17
Flush draw

Your hand
     QUEEN   EIGHT
     DIAMONDS   DIAMONDS

The flop
     ACE   NINE   SIX
     DIAMONDS   CLUBS   DIAMONDS

You need a diamond to complete the flush.

You have a total of nine outs:

On the turn   (9 / 47) = 19.1%
On the river   (9 / 46) = 19.6%
    Total   = **38.7%**

So you have a 38.7% chance of completing the flush on the turn or river. These are very good odds with a payback number of 2.6:1.

Example 18
Flush draw plus a pair

Your hand
> QUEEN   EIGHT
> DIAMONDS   DIAMONDS

The flop
> ACE   EIGHT   SIX
> DIAMONDS   HEARTS   DIAMONDS

With the addition of a pair to your flush draw, now you have a total of fourteen outs for improving your hand:

Complete the flush	nine outs	(you need any Diamond)
Complete the set	two outs	(you need any Eight)
Second pair	three outs	(you need any Queen)

What is the total probability of improving your hand?

On the turn	(14 / 47) = 29.7%	
On the river	(14 / 46) = 30.4%	
Total	= **60.1%**	

So the total probability of improving your hand is 60.1%. These are excellent odds, with a payback number of 1.7:1.

Example 19
Open-ended straight draw plus flush draw

This is a very powerful hand with excellent odds of completion.

Your hand
QUEEN   TEN
CLUBS   CLUBS

The flop
JACK   NINE   SIX
CLUBS   HEARTS   CLUBS

You have a total of seventeen outs to complete the flush or the straight:

Complete the flush   Nine outs (any club)
Complete the straight   Eight outs (a King or Eight)

What is the probability of completing either?

On the turn   (17 / 47) = 36.1%
On the river   (17 / 46) = 36.9%
   Total   = **73.0%**

So the total probability of your catching the straight or the flush is 73%. These are the best odds of any possible draw hand in Texas Hold'em. The payback number is very low at 1.4:1.

Example 20 A
Completing a full house (two pair on the flop)

Your hand
      JACK   TEN
      DIAMONDS   SPADES

The flop
      JACK   TEN   EIGHT
      CLUBS   HEARTS   CLUBS

You have flopped two pair, but there is a concern here that someone might have a straight or be on a straight or flush draw.

What is the probability of completing the full house?

You have a total of four outs on the turn, two Jacks and two Tens. You also have a total of seven outs on the river, because now you can also match the turn card:

On the turn   (4 / 47) = 8.5%
On the river   (7 / 46) = 15.2%
   Total   = **23.7%**

So the total probability of completing the full house is 23.7%. The payback number is 4.2:1.

Example 20 B
Completing a full house (through a set on the flop)

Your hand
JACK   TEN
DIAMONDS   CLUBS

The flop
JACK   JACK   EIGHT
CLUBS   HEARTS   CLUBS

You have flopped a set, but maybe you are up against a flush draw.

What is the probability of completing the full house?

You have a total of six outs on the turn, either a Ten or an Eight. You also have a total of nine outs on the river, because now you can also match the turn card.

Please note that the probability of completing a full house when you have three of a kind after the flop via either a pair in your hand or by matching two of your player cards is the same.

On the turn   (6 / 47) = 12.8%
On the river   (9 / 46) = 19.5%
  Total   = **32.3%**

So the total probability of your catching the full house is 32.3%. The payback number is 3.1:1.

Summary

The game of Texas Hold'em poker has many different strategies and variations. There is no standard protocol or approach on how to play the game, but knowing the probabilities provided in this book should help you make the right decision most of the time.

These probabilities will provide you with an extra advantage and tool. For instance, you are playing the Ace/King hand knowing that the probability that you will match the Ace or King is at 63% is very helpful. You are holding a pocket pair knowing that the probability of hitting a set is at 20.7% should also be very helpful. You are holding a pocket pair, (pair of Tens as shown in example 3) and there are two higher cards in the flop, knowing that there is a 50% mathematical probability that one of your opponents is holding one of the cards that beats your hand will assist you in making your decision whether to call or fold. And say you are on an open-ended straight and flush draw after the flop. Knowing that you have a 73% chance of completing either the straight or the flush is definitely valuable for when it comes time to bet or call someone's bet.

These probabilities are not intended to replace your gut instinct or your read on your opponent. They are only intended to provide you with that extra advantage so you can hopefully come out ahead in your next session.

Good luck, and see you out there.

Notes